Free Roses

Chelsea Lynn LaBate

MEZCALITA
PRESS

FIRST EDITION, 2023 – 3rd Printing
Copyright © 2023 by Chelsea Lynn LaBate
All Rights Reserved
ISBN-13: 978-1-7348692-7-9

Library of Congress
Control Number: 2023934932

Cover Design: Jay Payne
Cover Photo: Nina Willoughby

MEZCALITA
PRESS

Mezcalita Press, LLC
Norman, Oklahoma

Free Roses

Chelsea Lynn LaBate

Table of Contents

Introduction

Shamans worldwide know that in order to understand
society and live more fully attuned to reality, they need
to go wild, travel out of their normal minds, and visit
the invisible world of Spirit, which is the undercurrent
of the visible world.

~ Aletheia Luna

In August 2019, seven months before the start of our
local lockdown, I was found in my house by the
Asheville police, naked, on the floor, on a white
blanket. I had fought the most epic battle of my life,
a battle of good and evil. It had stretched out over
four grueling days.

I had set traps, sung, danced, cried, strategized and
prayed. I met spirits from the far edges of the world
who had come to help me in my struggle. I didn't
sleep, I didn't eat, I didn't drink. Every night I laid
down and waited for the birds to sing. The bad guys
were coming, but the good guys were coming too.
And I didn't know who would get there first. I shook
in fear. Every morning was just one more day I got
to be alive.

Since surviving this...I have had three other
episodes. Healing from them has taken time. But
through it all, I have never abandoned the necessity
of this book. I kept writing. And writing, and writing.

Some of these poems were drafted with blue crayons in green-walled wards, where pens and pencils are considered weapons. I wrote both before and after the hospitalizations, and during the darkest hours of the pandemic, never leaving my station.

As all of this unfolded, I began to tap into the verifiably unseen. Though I am not a shaman, this ability—some would call it a "gift"—is often attributed to them. For me, the imbalanced state, the physical impact and accompanying horror, were not worth the "gift."

In this book you are holding, you will learn about the depths of my experience, and the moving parts of its ecstatic madness—when I had a direct line to the universe and all of its inhabitants.

Having had this view of the spirit world, I do not accept the visible world as the only truth. I believe there is, instead, an underlying current affecting all that we see. It was through connecting to this very energy—sometimes dark, sometimes beautifully luminous—that I was able to write these poems.

Acknowledgements

I would like to thank my parents, Susi and Russ White, for their care during and after my psychotic episodes. Many of these poems were written at their kitchen table during my recovery months. They gave me shelter, food and love – three things that others with my condition do not always have post hospitalizations.

I'd like to thank my dear friends Melissa Hyman, Jesse Ruth, Lucho Gomez, Ian Wilkinson, Angie Fornof, Alex Krug, Robert Aguilar, Erin Ufert, Gina Caldwell, Ashana Rose Michaels, Valorie Miller, and Quetzal Jordan for picking up my calls both in and out of the ward.

I'd also like to thank Nathan Brown and Grant Peeples for believing in this work and helping this project get to print and in the hands of family, friends and fans.

And finally I'd like to thank my yoga teacher, Michael Johnson, who shared the words of Krishna Das "Practice while you can, you'll need it when you can't." It was through his masterful daily classes in person, and virtually that I was able to meet the darkness with dignity and grace.

Free Roses

MEZCALITA
PRESS

SOMETHING IS TRYING
TO KEEP US TOGETHER

Something is trying to keep us together
because everywhere I go, there you are.

What are the chances we would meet
on a green mountain in Appalachia
tangled with rhododendron,
whipped by fragrant wind,
then find ourselves
on a rhinestone studded sea
sipping silver needle tea,
flushed with fuchsia sunsets?

How did you find me
on the drenched streets of Paris,
peddling a bicycle up that great hill
into the spinning blades
of The Moulin Rouge,
my red velvet blazer unbuttoned,
a poem bleeding blue in its left pocket?

Then again you found me
in the yellow-gold sands of Morocco
disguised as the camel's feet.

Funny you should appear as the star
in my dreams when I thought my
exhaustion from living would plague me
with nights of eternal darkness.

And is that you in the feathers of my breath
whispering the songs of endangered birds?

Strange how when I tell no one
where I am going, I sense you behind me
flanked at my shoulders,
guiding me like two great wings.

But tell me, do I have permission
to love you in return? May I kiss the feet
of You who does not have feet? May I embrace
the body of You who does not have form?
May I hold hands with your Holy Handlessness?

Your love is making a lunatic of me!
Bowing to palm trees,
kissing the wet mouth of lakes,
holding hands with shimmering
swords of sunlight.

One can only hope—
to those with conventional rituals
who need God to have a beard
or a bible or a building—
that these raw and spontaneous
acts of devotion
will simply appear
as dance.

I'VE BEEN TOLD

I've been told
angels have landed on Earth
somewhere in Italy
carrying roses of light
chanting Ave Maria in a key
no one has ever heard before.

I've been told
togetherness will build
the new global federation,
circles are softer than grids,
all Romes burn to reveal
the clearest rooms of heaven.

I've been told
there is great love in death,
that hearts print the highest currency
and grass and poets and sun
will always shine in
where the politicians and media
have failed us all.

I've been told we have family
in the black slates of space,
and lodged in the gelatinous
pockets of our cells,
but only in profound stillness
can we hear them.

I've been told
hoarding leads to calcification,
panic to flames,
opinions to hardness,
but laughter is the balm
against such behaviors.

I've been told
we came here to dance,
and if the beat never changed,
we'd never learn
new moves.

Who Drugged the Messenger?

Leave it to my psychiatrist
to prescribe a life sentence of poison
for riding the rainbow bridge too hard
between immaculate worlds.

The initial trip is always a deep hit
for commoners and family members
who confuse awakening with lunacy.

The "doctors" have no education
on third eyes, invisible ears or
inaudible symphonies.

I don't know what field they stand in,
but they will soon be alone
when all of the children are freed
and we have no more need
for their "medicine."

But let us remember,
even this padded cell has a door -
How do you think they got me in here?
My work as a messenger is to remind you
that every box has an opening.

Divine Intelligence lives
everywhere on Earth,
though it seems to be utterly
lacking in this "hospital."

Poet, scribe, seer...
My sentence was lighter this time.
My scrolls were not destroyed.
My captors even expressed care.

Still, no one can make me eat
that purple chicken in the cafeteria,
just like I can't force you to believe
this Great Ending we're living
is the beginning of all beginnings,
beginnings like we have never known.

At What Point

At what point
do we unveil deep
rhythms within rhythms,
songs within songs,
angelic messages coded
in the black bones of the media,
the barcodes of cereal boxes,
the flowered patterns of toilet paper
IT'S TIME TO COME HOME?

At what point
does the door knob buckle and weep,
confess it's never been accused
of spreading such threats,
lament softly, it was merely made
to help open doors?

At what point
do we find ourselves
swollen with time
but starving for group embrace?

At what point
do we realize
we've built houses from fear
that there wouldn't be enough
when there's always enough
despite faulty distribution?

At what point
do we broadcast
backyard chickens
sustain life better than politicians,
frogs should be crowned for their
surround sound serenading,
and every fruit tree
is a silent Queen
selfishly providing for her
unmet children?

At what point
do the days shed their
Earth given names,
hours their confined glasses,
minutes the harsh hashmarks
of their numbers,
to reveal the ancient time keeper
of your breath?

At what point
does tenderness triumph over hardness,
thoroughness over speed,
clarity over pollution,
service over ego,
innovation over greed?

At what point
will *we* replace *me?*

At what point
will white flags release us
back into the streets
to find the black seeds
of one another's eyes,
the ballads of neighborhood voices,
the wealth in each other's touch?

Two Raccoons Shoot Hoops

Two raccoons under quarantine agreed
"We should get outta the den,
go shoot some hoops."
They borrowed a ball from
a vertically blessed neighbor,
baptized it with alcohol wipes, and
walked to a secret park.

They spent the afternoon squinting into
the sun launching the impenetrable fruit
at impossible heights up to a rusty halo hoop.

They cursed at one another,
"You tripped me with your tail, man!"
"Oh yah, well your hands are too small!"
"You can steal better than you can dunk!"

Then they called each other names
my pen would not agree to report.

My point is, pay attention to the ways
we were designed to come together.

Some of us, who walk low to the ground
and crave the color of night should only
invite each other to go bowling.

~ *for Grant Peeples*

FREE ROSES

Someone took a long stick
made of fear or love,
we still can't tell,

poked us good
into the dark pits
of our caves,
took our names,
promised to give us new ones
someday...

Our homes became nests,
became prisons, became wards
then nests.

Silence came as relief,
as punishment, then as rest.

Solitude pried open the gates
to heaven, then to hell.
We dug deep into our memories,
into timelines that curled like spirals
into the navel of source.

We remembered the bee
for its yellow-black suit,
then for its sting.

We tidied our lists of good
and bad and good and never again.

We found romance
in the original garden,
then boycotted it for its snakes,
then crawled back scrounging
for sour fruits.

We hung mirrors that reflected the light,
then shunned it for its lies,
then praised it for its accuracies.

We worshipped the sun
then blamed it for our burns
then thanked it for warming our seed.

We overdosed on making love
until we accused the other
of taking up space,
then took them back,
then pushed them away,
but lacked enough room.

We cuddled books then
longed for voices,
we listened to voices then craved
the place of no words.

We sang songs that elevated us
then wore us out,
left us bare as thread,
and hungry for touch.

Friends –
I have died a thousand times,
in tombs and in fields,
in crowds and alone.

I know now that anything material
has the power to house god
or the force that fears it.

So just imagine what business is like
for those of us who have come around,
again and again and again,
to stand on the street corners
and hand out free roses.

DOING NOTHING

I don't know how I missed your call
or that Virtual World Wide Hugging Event
or overlooked those two chin hairs
curled with all of the mystery of the cosmos
like a tiny copy of the Torah
on the spear of my chin.

I don't know how I forgot
to check the mail
when it may injure or kill me
if I don't lay it out
in the sun for three days –
an eternity in quarantine time.

I don't know how I keep forgetting
to do *that thing* that isn't fun,
now that I have all the time in the world.

I don't know what my day filled up with.
I remember the first chirp of morning,
looking for a lost shoe, crying then laughing,
half a panic attack after the disappearing act
of that *last piece of chocolate.*

I'm not sure how I wasn't around
to listen to all of your troubles
or trouble you with mine.
I have no more fingernails to chew.

I don't know how I didn't get around
to folding this week's laundry,
educating myself on governments
and global warming,
or building something new out of an old fear
that there won't be enough.

I guess I was busy
doing nothing.

THE UGLY ONES

This morning I rose,
sipped the sweet ambrosia of awakening,
drew in the song of the dawn,
bowed and blushed.
Then the waters presented
a thousand diamond rings of light.

I gave thanks for the grand and the clean,
for the unseen and eternal.

The Voice leaned in and smiled,
"That's good little lotus,
but have you thanked the ugly ones?"

"Remember to sing for your executioner
as she paces down the hall to escort you
to your death."

"Give away your finest dresses to the jealous,
who make it their work to burn you
in the community square."

"Save your purest words for the blind
and the violent."

"Plant chrysanthemums around
the unmarked tomb
where they plan to bury you,

leave a mark of beauty
where your blood will pool."

"You will rise again."

"Be sure to ask your crucifier
how his day has been
as he escorts you up to the cross."

"Offer that one last loaf
to those who have robbed you,
cleaned your house,
done you the honor
of separating the fakers
from the true,
the needed from the excess,
the loud from the crooked,
the finite from the eternal."

"Love is easy to love,
so remember to love the ugly ones.
Only then can we all go home."

FINISH LINE

This morning my walk
took twice as long.

Moved by inaudible song,
I shook and contorted,
shimmied and swooped,
bent and bowed.

I became the village madwoman.

This body has never liked
to move on a straight track.

As I moved I felt
I could walk for twenty-seven days,
sweating with ecstasy,
humbled by the simplicity
of coming into contact
with a supreme, melodic power.

Tell me Sweet Dancers,
in these moments are *we* dancing,
or is something grander dancing us?

Do you use the same moves to invite the angels in
as you do to escort the demons out?
If so, is this why crying sometimes sounds
like laughing?

As I moved through the woods I prayed,

Oh lord above,
oh lord inside of me,
keep my sword sharp
and my song sweet
so that I may navigate
this unpredictable story
with you by my side.

A great peace washed over me.
I kept walking,
forgetting where I would end.
Then a great symphony swooped down
from the branches above.
I was bathed in songs.

Why be concerned
with the destination
when God is your DJ?

~ for Erin McAlister Ufert

INHALE

The first time I was decapitated,
butterflies of light
flew from my throat
and fluttered over the fields of Italy.

When I was burned at the stake,
the ashes of my sisters and I
fertilized the ground with songs
that I sometimes still catch
children humming.

When I was hung from a willow tree,
the birds couldn't bare the sight
of such a strange fruit
and slipped into a collective silence
that amplified the moonlight.

When I was shot in civil war,
the red bars of the flag washed white,
and just before I passed,
every hand-stitched star
became the Star of Bethlehem.

When I was crucified,
my body became bread,
my blood a river of wine.

When I was drowned,
the bubbles became pearls

that still appear in my hair
when I'm bathing.

In Vietnam, I set myself on fire
then reincarnated and prayed
"Please give me the strength
to love those who are sick
enough to kill a child of God."

Every murder hurts The Great Mother
and all of her creatures.

Let's honor suffering with a deep inhalation.

May the stolen breath of God's children
propel the wings of the angels.

May the horror of every unjust death
be the ink that writes humanity
into the New Era of Peace.

~ for George Floyd

THE PINE TREE IS STILL OPEN FOR BUSINESS

The pine tree is still open for business
and happily receiving guests
of all shapes and color.

It says no one will be turned away
for having a beak too dull,
or a tail too scrawny,
a feather too ordinary,
or a squawk too loud.

And as for you small crawlers,
you are *all* welcome despite
your number of uncountable legs.

The grass is still bending
under fleshy boned feet,
the rubbered wheels of a wagon,
the flat mat of a midday blanket,
a warm lump of dog poo.

The lake is still committed to mimicking
the mutating expressions of clouds.
The crickets show up to rehearse
in their cacophonic choirs.

The monarchs cut the air
with pollen dusted prayers
and the wildflowers dispatch
the good news of the wind.

The lizards spy on all who are
giving, dying and beginning,
and prepare their reports
for the Master of Balance.

The sun still shines
on the ignorant and the weak,
on the hopeful and the numb,
on the ecstatic and the grateful.

Who pays it? *None of us know.*

There must be worlds within worlds
within worlds within worlds.

Someone said the world has shut down,
stopped, closed, cerado, fermée, caput!
But the pine tree is still open for business.

UNEMPLOYED ARTISTS

Most artists are not employed
yet pull miracles out of nothing,
fool the masses,
trick everyone into thinking
there has been some sort of
sponsorship.

Most artists are used to worrying
about the ever-approaching rent,
getting down to that last
frozen pizza, panicking –
will that one swinging bulb
above them stay on?

Most artists give all
for a distracted applause,
a few stale crumbs,
a little blue "Like" earned
while viewers take a dump.

Most artists have no problem
reporting to their studios.

Most artists are used to using
lemons instead of health care,
prayer instead of savings,
friends instead of insurance.

Most artists believe
weed, paint, guitar strings and moonlight
are far more important
than bathroom supplies.

Most artists don't believe
governments will save them,
that they'll just have to do it themselves
because they always do it themselves.

Most artists are guilty of printing
a bicycle on a tea towel or performing
Wagon Wheel so they can eat.
Most artists are smarter than the work
they make for others.

Some artists make for an audience
who haven't been born yet.

Most artists are polite –
don't rub it in
that what they give actually
costs them,
so that humanity will have a reason
to wake up, have a weekend, live.

Most artists are used to going without,
though they are intelligent enough,
hard working enough,

driven enough,
to have everything.

Maybe now that this pandemic
has graced us,
YOU can be an artist too!

ONLY MY GOOD FRIENDS KNOW

Today I wore my satin prom dress
to fetch the mail,
threw my arms out
like an unleashed watering hose,
bellowed *Dancing Cheek to Cheek*
in soft longing.
I tossed the split ends of my hair
back, pinched up my gloves,
shuffled through bills
that would not be paid
anytime soon.

Today I invented recipes,
dusted cantaloupe with
brown freckles of cinnamon,
tried frying a cloud of cottage cheese,
married peanut butter to the pea.

Today I sang all of Elvis Presley's top hits
to our most demanding house cat
who blinked and said
"the acoustics are better in the bathroom,
and you should really drink more water."

Today I considered that not all artists
need crisis to make good art,
but all artists need to know how good
they are for others in crisis.

Today I rode my bike through empty streets
in a cheetah spotted onesie and yelled
"You will never domesticate meeeeEEEeEee!"

Today I questioned why some
make death out to be so serious.

Today I practiced my whistling,
jazz crackling on a 99 cent radio
while I clipped my toenails
in a shed that I share
with salamanders.

Today I stopped using toilet paper
on behalf of the trees
and the American people,
I just peed outside,
then French kissed a pine.

Today my cup was half full.

Today I rearranged my books in rainbow order
but got confused about blacks and whites
so gave up, then consulted my brother
on prime methods of sock folding,
and purged anything that made me
feel stuck and small.

Today I found angels in wallpaper patterns,
nervous bunnies in dustballs,
anxious faces in light sockets
and re-assured them all "we're okay."

Today I prayed for those who step
into flood and flames they may
have trouble finding names for
and considered that maybe
that's why scientists catalogue with numbers.

Today I responded to only those who have
my true well-being in mind,
who know my back stories,
who value me simply for being kind.

Today I freed a lizard from the gridded grip
of the window screen only to find
he had come back to self-quarantine.

Which of these happened because
the world has to stay home now?

"Only my good friends know."

SOCIAL DISTANCING

I asked our dogs to
"please give me some distance!"
while I peed outside.

They didn't.

Instead they circled around
in wild ceremony gnawing,
mashing and stomping
licking lips, dragging branches,
snorting and chanting
"Pee! Pee! Pee! Pee!"

The little black one stamped my third eye
with the wet wand of her nose.
The mustard one whipped me in the ear
with a tail ruled by primal ecstasy.
The brown one huffed puffs
of moist turkey breath
into the bowls of my nostrils.

I had heard once that some tribes
have no word for "privacy."

As I rolled down my skirt,
I began to suspect
that they lacked words
for other things like

"hurry" or "tomorrow,"
"evil" and "death."

As we walked in to yet
another quarantine sunset,
I pondered – What words
could humans forget
to come home?

~ *for Nico, Molly and Paulo*

LIVE AUDIENCE

This morning I informed my cat
that I would no longer be improvising
sing-along-songs for him
during lock down.

He glared at me as though
he had forgotten all human language.

"That one about the little sardines in a basket
kept me up all night!" I explained,
two dark moons drooped down my face.

He shook his head, studied the
illuminated fur of his dingle ball feet.
"Masterpiece," he said,
"It was a Masterpiece."

"I can't do it," I begged.
"It just kept looping and looping.
We'll have to go back to ballads –
songs that are long and slow,
something I can fall asleep to
in case it gets stuck."

Silence. Two slits for eyes.

Since then, he's been confined
to his cardboard box.
He doesn't even move an ear

when I walk through.
He only sits up to crunch dried food,
stare out the window,
wonder if joy will ever move
through the tiny bones
of his body again
while I am left to starve
for the attention
of my most loving
live audience.

THE REAL SONG

The Real Song plays on after death.
The Real Song lives on the lips of everyone.
The Real Song comes out in spurts and fragments.
The Real Song has a thousand tongues.

The Real Song never makes slaves of its makers.
The Real Song is our closest companion.
The Real Song lives in unseen kingdoms.
The Real Song ruptures like thunder.

The Real Song rises from the moist
mouths of lovers.
The Real Song was never born.
The Real Song can be passed
from insect to human.
The Real Song can never be owned.

The Real Song comes out in gold and gray,
checkerboard or zigzag.
The Real Song is only love, sometimes
ecstasy, sometimes madness.
The Real Song travels on light beams and trash.
The Real Song ties hearts together
with invisible ribbons.

The Real Song fights off psychic predators.
The Real Song kept me alive in the ward.
The Real Song feeds all life sustaining seeds.
The Real Song fills your pockets.

The Real Song claims all balconies in crisis.
The Real Song is awake or asleep.
The Real Song never apologizes
for incomplete deliveries.
The Real Song restores planet, galaxy and nebula.

The Real Song moves in waves and circles.
The Real Song cannot be mispronounced
or imprisoned.
The Real Song does not fear the darkest hour.
The Real Song brings all soldiers of war home.

The Real Song will never hurt you.
The Real Song was not made to sell beer
or make false kings out of greedy,
suit-wearing commoners.
The Real Song does not excuse its volume,
size or beauty.
The Real Song never forgets and cannot be
forgotten.

The Real Song does not need an electrical outlet.
The Real Song will never need a cab ride home.
The Real Song can be heard with the ears
inside your ears.
The Real Song will always serve and never ends.

MADNESS

On my way to madness
I took off my housedress,
left it loosely arranged
like a donut
on the floor
where I thought
I would die alone.

Then I leapt,
not out the window,
but to the next room
where I was found
by officers and neighbors
naked on a puffed, white blanket,
swollen with victory
still stuttering to God.

The battle had been won
between light and evil,
predator and victim,
snake and dove.

I had been deeply afraid,
but when I pressed palms with death,
I found myself in great company.

Does an alarm sound in the heavens
when a child of the Earth
is approaching the gates?

Who curates the unseen team
that guides us beyond?

I purged the house,
littered the lawn with
a thousand glittering buttons,
drowned books in garbage pails,
laid out old clothes as bait
for the demons.

I was instructed to run fans
to scramble my scent,
stack hangers as traps,
cover every black hole
that could be used by spies.

Reflective surfaces
became aid to keep watch.
Dance was a release.
Blue flowered shawls draped me
in the Holy Mother's protection.

Now in my sane mind I ask –
When does medicine become addiction?
Creativity, delusion?
Imagination, mania?

Is trauma the gateway to enlightenment?

How can the cries of our ancestors
be soothed if we don't fall through
dimensions to sing beyond the veil?

And how will we ever shake loose
that which is plaguing us
if we are afraid
to worship wildly
in a house
which is seldom visited?

Highly Contagious

Two crickets sat on a log watching
another quarantine sunset.

"Haven't seen many humans out,"
the younger one said.
"Something's going around, it's highly contagious."

"I heard you catch it by hearing a baby laugh,
being kind to your neighbors or by sitting
for long periods of time in one place."

"I heard you get it from group hugging,
feeding one another and caring for the sick."

"There's a study saying it may travel on
hand written letters, music and eye contact."

"Oh, that powerful, huh?" Said the elder.

"Someone told me it may travel on sunlight,
water and dirt, but that it could be the flowers
transmitting it—their color and velvety texture."

"What happens if you catch it?"
Asked the young one.

"Oh, you may wander out into the streets,
hand all your money to strangers,

sing to the unseen, whirl in circles,
lose all fear of death."

"It sounds like we may not stand a chance,"
said the young one.

"I've never seen anything like this in my lifetime,"
said the elder.

As the last drops of daylight
shattered across the water,
like an army of golden worms, they pulled out
their fiddles and positioned their bows.

"We better be prepared."

THE ROOSTER

When asked about loyalty
and his role as a man,
The Rooster, with his swooping tail
of iridescent jewel-toned feathers says –
"The hens are my world.
My heart gets so full
I can barely make it to dawn.
I just have to sing
thinking of their sweetness
and their humble chirps."

Unaccustomed to interviews,
he extends his neck to check his flock.

"Every morning they wake up
filled with yellow suns,
but I am the same,
I am nothing next to them.
I crow. I chase off snakes.
I eat a questionable spider
that may do them harm,
but they house the mystery of the cosmos."

I've known a few men to speak like this
who are consumed with grace,
who live to protect the Great One's beauty
in whichever form it comes.

Perhaps there are many more
wanting to devote their lives to those
who give their whole life
to birthing eternal light.

Now that the empire is crumbling
we'll have to let them know
the Original Service is hiring again.

They can quit their life of false priorities,
leave their screens and cells,
come home to their thrones.

HER

In the springs she appears,
smooth as sunshine,
hair a slick of yellow-white,
cheeks like golden apples,
casually swimming against
the cold water current.

As she floats, the Great Oaks
veil her with their green-gray shadows
careful not to contaminate her song.

I have returned
lifetime after lifetime
to give myself to "her,"
to her silky elegance,
to her inaudible laughter.

Inside of me is an unrecognizable shape
which always points me in her direction.

I paddle in her shimmering wake and pray
"Everything I've ever done is for you!
I've come here again and again for you!
I've burned in the bluest flame for you!"

I keep my distance, engulfed in her beauty.

All others move with the current
on their plastics devices,

full of hot dogs from the concession stand
shrieking and splashing.

Jesus is my brother.
His mother was Mary.
She had a Mother who had a Mother
But all Mothers come from "her."

She cannot be named.
Religions shrink in her presence.

All that blocks, controls,
dismantles and stains,
will be outshined by her grace.

TODAY I ASKED THE BUTTERFLY

Today I asked the butterfly
what it's like to be a butterfly.
She perched on the purple skirt
of a petunia and asked –
"What's a butterfly?"

I blushed with shame
at the notion of assigning a name
to someone who never named herself,
someone who is so absorbed in being
that she doesn't need identity.

I started to move in ways
I had never moved before.
Losing my name meant
I could become the unknown,
a pattern, an echo, a prayer.

I mimicked the bear, the great moose,
the rhino, the squirrel.
I morphed and shifted,
but when I thought of the butterfly
I felt the most uplifted.

I didn't know the God in me
until I became the small,
winged one who drinks from
the hearts of flowers.

ONE GOOD TEACHER

Sometimes Masters of the Galaxy
disguise themselves as locusts,
wind, frogs or yoga instructors.
A good student knows
when one has appeared,
suddenly on the path.

In the months before my Awakening
I listened to every word my teacher said,
inverted my body, steadied my breath.
He corrected my footing, pillowed my eyes
helped make my stance *strong*.

I sat for hours in meditation,
ordered my mind to play with nothing
but breath and sacred word.

I could have gone on as before
with my walls full of scriptures,
with my worn out familiar guides
and tattered odysseys,
with my already accomplished missions.

But he appeared,
with his steadiness and equanimity,
his tenderness and care,
to help me ascend.

Sometimes, to the untrained eye,
grace looks like unskilled chaos.
Sometimes the challenge
is to simply untangle from
what has been binding you.
Other times it's knowing when to dance
in the company of a Master.

Thanks to him my senses are more liberated.
The rainbow has 64 colors now.

I've crossed over to the present moment
where all thoughts are servants to beauty
and knowledge is free.

~ *for Michael Johnson*

SURFIN' USA

The last time I occupied the ocean
I paddled freely right to the main room.
There was no hallway, no door,
I didn't even have to break glass
to access her.

She immediately recognized me
as one of her own, yet did not force me
into any limiting citizenship.
My friends were there too,
strong shouldered, unidentified
and sparkling with salt.

We're safer here.
Bad news can't travel across clean lines.
It's impossible.

Pathways built by beauty
have their own frequent flyers.
Any of us can have access that
even angels dream of.
No need to get distracted by children starting fires.

Spirals sustain life, squares contain it.
What is there to react to if you're already included?

After an afternoon of catching waves
I exited the Atlantic full and missing nothing.
A fiddler crab crossed by my path nervously

and reported the news from The Mainland –
"The upset ones are throwing rocks again.
This time there is unrest in the capitol."

I thanked him for his service
then paddled back out
amongst the black finned sharks
and the man-o-war,
the dolphin and the osprey,
to that place where
nothing is secure
and everyone is free.

INVISIBLE MOVEMENT

Someone just informed me
we still have a government here.
I've been working hard tending
a revolution with no form.

Some movements are so subtle
they are thin as spiders webs,
their power nearly invisible,
their maps drawn by night.

I know who my fellow spinners are.
I spot them in the village,
disguised as checkout clerks
and selling gas.

We are all reporting to our stations
in cities and on coastlines,
waiting for the moment
to remove our full body masks.

Don't worry, the New Dawn is here.
You'll get the change you've been living for,
though it may not look like victory.

The freedom to live is non-sensational
and made up of steady, loyal tasks.

Yes, when you inhabit the untrue spaces
you'll forget about elections,

good and bad,
or what ballot you cast.

Because the power of the people
is in the light of remembering
no empire can contain
what was built to last.

A LITTLE DIFFERENT THIS TIME

Every time I come to Earth
I drink the elixir,
forget ancient scripture,
put on the heavy suit.

I let the village of fools
talk over me,
wear their masks,
charge high admission
to their freak shows.

I wander the edges,
sing from broken ledges,
get tossed between pearl and thorn.
I tread dark waters,
trade diamonds for quarters,
pull down memos from the moon.

Every messenger knows there is great
risk in attempting to deconstruct
old empires with the word.
Even my own family thinks I'm sick

for reporting on things no one else can see –
but this role is nothing new,
we've been doing it since the beginning,
presenting truth that threatens change.

Trust me, I can see what I can see.
There is a rainbow rolling out before us
and things are going to play out
a little different this time.

THANK DOG

Thank dog I have animals
to talk to out loud,
in public squares
and in cluttered kitchens,
on worn wooden porches
and on crooked windowsills.

I can stretch my voice down low
in a *boh-woah, boh-woah*
or sculpt it into a point
with an *eee-eee, eee-ee.*

I can pinch the steeple
of their furry heads while doing
an oompah dance, or sing a song
about pee and then rhyme it
with "wild and free."

Without them,
I'd be hauled off again
to that *not fun place,*
be discharged with the diagnosis
of being multi-lingual
or as some doctors call it
schizophrenic.

Instead, my buddies
accommodate me
through the realm

of the masked and misled
so that I may have
"acceptable" outbursts
of playing with God.

YIN-YANG

I'm too sober for this part –
this part where intensive yoga
turns on my magical thinking
and all enemies, in hindsight,
become highly prized teachers.

My insignia is invisible, as are all
titles and ranks in this Army of Grace.

Today on my walk, a yin-yang appeared
and hovered just before me.
It said, "Black has a heart of white light."
"Does light have a black heart?," I asked.
"No, it merely carries it in a protected place
so it may share the moves of non-violence."

Then the dots slid out and multiplied
on a flat board, clusters of black
"attacked" white light by surrounding it,
but nearby white surrounded black
and flipped it to white,
making it one of its own.

"But black must always be identified as black,"
the voice noted, "or you'll go crazy, you see?"

"I'm talking to a symbol," I noted.

"You've got a good point," it confirmed.

All parts are related.
All children of god are invited to dance.
But you must understand the recipes for change.

Anger is never love.
Blame is never progress.
Killing does not mean an end.
Stealing is never earning.
Hatred is never kindness.
But all of God's creations move as one.

I bowed and thanked my teacher.
A sheet of warm, yellow sun unfolded before us
and a cluster of periwinkle butterflies
lifted from their station.

The path before me was smooth and vacant.
It welcomed all decisions and digressions.

NEW SONG

Play that New Song again –
the one with the base line that sparks kissing.
My dress is torn in a thousand places
but I'll have to make do,
you know I always do.

Somehow somewhere someone
will recognize the beauty in me –
the parts that were fought for,
all extra components sold off for loose change.

Please stop calling it mental illness.
The mind is fine though the psyche is tattered.
We rainbows battle for colors
even we can't see, colors we'll need
to cross over the Great Bridge
with grace, faith and determination.

Not all couriers are insane.
We deliver messages
we can't translate or understand
but recognize their value by the way
their letters bend the light.

Leave it to the ones you need the most
to never admit they are struggling,
to be that lighthouse,
to consistently provide a signal
when your bow is slapping rock.

I met a robin this morning
its breast round with melody.
It sang proud and sweetly.

"There's nothing to fear.
We will now rise to sing
the song of the New Earth."

TOMORROW, A VICTORY

Tomorrow is always a victory
for those of us who have returned
again and again to fight the true fight.

We know the long nights
standing alone on our star-spoked podiums
clutching one good book for courage,
our right arm buckling under a heavy torch.

No one knows the darkness
of near death
until you've stood in the possibility
of not seeing the dawn.

So stay up all night if you have to.
Befriend the tunnel that haunts you.
Spend your last reserve of life force
tending your tender flame.

And know there are millions of others
burning in their holders
fueled by Liberty,
oriented towards the East.

Some change is so Big
government can't contain it,
and with the break of dawn
the people will rise up to rip out the wiring
and take the shape of lighting in the streets.

TURTLE SAYS

On my walks, turtle appears –
smooth and slippery-black on a log,
stacked in plastic on green lawn decorations,
scurrying into a sandy hole.

"What is it turtle?," I ask
      "Too fast," turtles says.

"If I was going any slower, I'd be dead!"
      "Dead slow, new fast."

The unseen has been hiding my pens from me,
setting my pace,
telling me not to rush
into any more toppling towers.

In this final hour, Dear Ones,
you may consider doing the same.

Instead of being employed, married,
or burdened by children,
I've found myself naked in the fields
sticky with sunlight,
empty as breath,
chanting The Mother's name.

To who's table have we been racing?
If you eat where you pray,
why would you ever have to commute to God?

Later a kind voice told me
"The mother is very sick."
One of the old oaks lit up
with blue strips of blinking lights
in a way only few of us can see.

"We've got the Elders on life support.
Your planet is so poisoned,
if it wasn't for galactic support,
you'd all be dead."

Sometimes the unreal becomes so real
a great silence rolls over the crowd
and shuts everyone up.

There is no debating divine reality.

The lords of ego, greed and fear
have done a number on us all.
But maybe, just maybe, we're going to see
how easy it will be to break free.

Songs of Silence

"It'll make a good song," some say
in response to my current situation
of being locked up
in a mental ward,
infested with broken hope.

To that I say, "It is not a messenger's job
to relay the intricacies of the ugly and persistent
with the blood of this pen."

"It could have been worse," some may say,
but you'll never know the terror –
the sad textures, the sour smells,
the night-screaming that shattered the halls
into a constellation of black stars.

God barely resides in such places.
The clock is a circle I wrestle with,
a clicking moon,
a numbered, shoo-fly pie.

$1500-a-day to eat purple chicken
off a Styrofoam plate.

No one to hug.

Now that I am out, it's a sweet reunion
with the blue-bodied butterfly

who finds its home on the bulb
of my big toe.

With the gurgle of rainwater
and its clear wrinkles in the gutters,
with the peach sherbet sky
penetrated by silver blinking radio towers,
with the pine tree's shimmering needles.

Some fires feed us,
some give off smokey hope,
some shape us into gemstones even
galactics find hard to believe are real.

No one can re-create
the technology of mortal recovery –
this human organism that sings
pulls magic from a library of other lifetimes,
celebrates tiny victories
even when housed by shadow.

How do we endure?

Silence is the ultimate song, my friends,
and in its clear, clear breath
we can hear the eternal choirs
of immaculate angels.

THE GREAT PAUSE

Today I walked on water again.

When I placed the fears
of our horrifying "future"
behind me, it pushed at my back,
as smooth crystalline wind.

I lifted and began to fly.

Flying is better than walking.
The body goes horizontal
as if dreaming or making love.
The feet don't tire,
the nose begins to steer in all directions.

Sometimes a teacher appears
to show you "The Way"
only to leave you to figure out
the path is rolling out of your own ass.

The last time I caught fire,
ripe with discovery,
I discovered that even in great heats
there is always a cool knob to hold on to.

Some like to say "We are all doing our best,"
but I know when I have resorted
into worm-like behaviors,
and when I am failing the collective.

I catch myself on the couch –
with its luxurious cats and cushions,
convinced "the world" doesn't need me,
that it's all an undo,
that we'll just wait for the call to alert us
when it's time to come out
and pick up the trash.

But all professional conductors
know the power of dead silence –
that Great Pause that tricks us
into thinking it's the end.

Then, a piccolo trills in,
like a hummingbird with metal wings
and in the golden drops of dawn sings,
"We have risen!"

FOUND

After three thousand lifetimes of searching,
I finally found a needle in a haystack.

When I pinched it in my fingers
and studied the silver sliver of its form,
the Great Wind blew from the West
and the needle landed in a pile of needles.

"My needle!," I shrieked.

The Voice just laughed.
"Now it's time to find the piece of hay!," it said.
Its cackling caused more wind.

Friends, all material life is here
to play a game with you,
to help you feel lost and hopeless,
so you may witness the ecstasy,
of finding what you never lost.

OFFERINGS

One day while walking through the deep woods
I came across the throne of an unseen
Queen and King.
In their seats, sat two silver moons of rainwater.

I gathered my skirt and knelt down.
I bowed my head forward
and presented a bouquet of pine needles
for the noble couple.

It is in these moments that I feel
the breath of God move through me.
These spells, these small rituals,
when God makes an offering to God
through God and all of creation
shifts and sighs.

Nature is a good church,
it reminds us that we are owned
by something large, shifting and magnificent
and we are given all the tools
to come back home.

We only need to be brave enough
to bow to the unguided and unnamed
in the name of The One,
who through silent suggestion,
is forever bowing to us.

THE BIG TIME

Some artists understand that
making it Big means remaining small.

In our youth we may have wanted
to be Giants—ambassadors of the airwaves,
professional colonizers of the internet,
penetrators of all hand held devices
all of them.

But who wants a life where fame
strips off ones' little pink
wings of autonomy?

You see,
all who are large and identifiable
must shrink down for safety,
scurry from back door to black car,
hideout, grow their hair,
shave their heads,
disguise their true selves,
write on their luggage tag
"The Milkman's Son."

In all my divine wanderings,
I was never asked by man or angel
to shrivel down into a pocket or corner.

But on my humble stages
if the wind is just right,

if I've been fed
and am full of clean water,
if I have the company
of neighbors and good friends,
if I am full of song and scripture,
my heart begins to glow.

It expands out of my mouth
into the microphone,
out of the little sound system,
under the open air and loquat trees
and covers the entire planet
and all of its creatures in love.

PROVIDER

Today I took a long, thin stick
and carved a good poem in the sand.

When the wet tongue of the sea
smeared its letters flat into shallow scars
I thought, "Hallelujah! I have finally made it!"

The seagulls must have heard
the thud of my heart,
the stomp of its little red valves,
and began to circle and squawk overhead
as if the victory of attaining nothingness
counted for something.

Who says all pages are paper?
Who says words need an alphabet?
Who says, that our greatest masterpieces
aren't logged into the shells and the stars
only to be swallowed
by The Great Mother
so that, happy and full,
she can go on providing
for all of her children?

TWINKLE

Who says a stick is just a stick?

In these woods I pick up a tree limb,
detached by storm, walk with it a bit
then offer it back to the Great Mother
who will use it to grow more life.

Every teacher is sacrificing itself
so that life can breed life.

What an honor to surrender shape.
How brave to renounce names.
How wondrous to discover boundaries
are merely an illusion.

I became liquid once.
I moved across smooth surfaces
like thought without form,
turned shapes into sound,
became a mirror for the heavens.

When the stars looked down they said –
"Look at us! We are songs!
We are guides! We are diamonds!"

And I, a reflection, became nothing.

HOLOGRAM

You are pure source in drag.
That's why I'm laughing under my mask
in this gas station jiffy store
where, through the eyes of my heart,
I see we're all one.

I must have drunk some strange syrup
that confused me, closed my third eye,
shrank my mind into believing
costumes and overcoats are dividing lines.
Nonsense.

You, as me, push a carton of Marlboros
across a slick red counter,
snap air to expand a bag
with two quick nods of your wrists,
announce the total in American dollars.

I'm in awe at your performance.
The separation is almost believable.

How many dividing lines will dissipate
during this Great Sleep?
How many Yous have I been?
How long will I love myself as you?

The Great Wheel is turning.
The old shadows are being
washed from this hologram,

and those of us who volunteered
to get boxed up, locked up
and drugged up are coming out

to help out just a little longer,
to see the dawn of the New Earth.

THIS PLACE

This place, where angels are sent to die.
This place, with its torn linoleum floors
and blinking bulbs yellow-white.
This place, with its flooding showers
and beige walls bleeding graffiti

    JESUS HAS RISEN
KISSES TO MY BITCHES
    GOODBYE 2020

This place, where I sing spontaneously
in a double line of inmates
draped in torn, baby blue hospital robes
nervously picking at plastic barcode bracelets
under a black skylight cross.

This place, where I sing to survive,
my voice floating up like feathers of light
from the pink, wet cave of my mouth.

A song leaves me like a white flag of surrender.
Our pod unravels its tendrils, its gnarled fists.
I give my melody freely.

The brother with the face tattoos shouts,
"Yo dog, she froze the nurses."
The lines look towards their station,
clipboards hovering in route,
name tags swinging to a stop.

This place, "Who is singing?!"
I remain tucked in the warmth of my tribe —
convicts and cutters, homeless and loony birds.

This place is seldom graced
by the gospel of kidnapped messengers,
brought here by shipwreck or disaster.
This place, where holiness can survive
in memory and under starlight.
This place, where darkness
sleeps inside darkness.

This place, I will leave, branded by the ugly
to a parking lot of gray cars,
to welcome a broken morning
and a new song of survival.

MIXED UP

Today on the trail
a beetle crossed my path and shouted
"You need to get your shit togetha!
You can't go walking around here
saying *this is that* and *up is down*.
You're gonna get yourself all
mixed up."

I stopped to listen and adjusted my cap,
not wanting to go to the bad place again,
the place where mystics are diagnosed insane.

"This is Earth and there are laws.
I'm a beetle. I'm not a princess or a savior
or a wagon, I'm a beetle and proud of it.
We beetles have been here some 30 million years.
I'm strong, raised good kids
and navigate by the milky way.
You, are human. Human, not a dolphin or a fairy.
You need water and food and sleep."

I wiped some sweat from my brow.

"A captain will never call the sky the sea,
or rename East and West. You see?
He'd get mixed up."

"But what about the saying as above, so below?"
I inquired.

"What about it? It's a *reflection*.
Don't go making trees clouds.
Earth and the heavens mirror each other.
You think an angel knows what it's like to put a
finger in the fire?
An actual finger? No."

"Am I imagining this?," I asked.
"Beetles don't talk."

"You need to get you ears cleaned out!
Of course we talk.
All of creation can talk to one another.
And I don't mean using a mouth
and those ears on the side of your head!"

"That's all for now," she said,
almost across the path.
"Your job is to keep some good
ground under your feet
and remember which way is UP."

"Okay, thank you," I said.
"We are all servants of good," she said.
"You know where to find me."

This Mess

If you can't love the president,
love your cat,
a house plant or a sunset.
Love something half-beautiful
broken or dull,
love your green field opponents
or a gas station tenant.

Unravel the soft purr of your heart
on something you're not afraid of,
something that won't throw rocks at you,
something that won't plague
your blood with animosity
towards your brothers,
a small love that will help you
feel whole again.

The Great War in the sky is over
and those of us who have stuck around
this long, sandbagging ourselves
to the Earth with the weight of
unfinished Karma, so that we don't
float away to another dimension,
are tired and want to go home.

But before we go,
we've gotta clean up this mess.

So let's clear the table
and set it for *everyone*,
including the leaders we built
collectively with our own
daily thoughts of hate.

No Fear

The last time
I didn't do my work
to accommodate
someone else's fear
was never.

Recently I can hear the true language
of the light, speak without words
in all forms, through every element
in this world and the next.

It can't be capped or edited to fit your frame.
It will break through, set bushes on fire,
spill off the tongues of "crazy" messengers like me,
even when the books have been destroyed.

If you're offended by uncertainty,
you'll soon find
we didn't come here to be comfortable.

So remember,
the only school that's needed
is the Great Heart.
You can leave the classroom,
follow the sun,
ask the crocodile to eat your clock.

The only law that is needed
comes from The Mother,

the sustainer of all life –
the raw genius of her organism.

Why are you listening to me?
Who needs a messenger when
you have a direct line?

Here I am coming out for you again.
I work for no one, I get paid nothing.

THE INVISIBLE

I'm writing to you
from the real world,
the one that floats inside
and all around you.
The one that can never be
bought nor sold.
The one that stays forever
undercover and out of the
grip of the foul and greedy.

I've bought a lot of stock
in the invisible,
made it my mission to marry
that which can never be
introduced in person
or documented by the five senses.

Our entire life is guided
by that which we cannot see,
that which moves
through sound and light,
that which travels on air and dream.

Yesterday, I sang to a willow tree.
Its dancing inspired the wind
to carry love notes
on the crescents of its leaves
to the lonely and the lost.

We messengers will always
present in the language
you can understand.
There are codes in fire,
sermons in your hair,
data in the dazzling diamond-
laced face of your backyard stream.

Our lines are being cleaned.
We are coming back into balance
with the song of the soul.

Here during this pandemic,
consciousness is stirring in all life.
You will not be left out.
The heart will not be defeated.

CLASSROOM

I've been split between homes
as long as I remember –
two of everything, one of something,
that get dragged between residencies
and galaxies, worn out or lost in transit.

My gardens become overgrown and go to seed.
Most friends are too far to touch,
especially the ones spun of starlight.

Some of my greatest teachers
instruct from the shadows.
It takes a sophisticated student
to be shaped by absence,
enter no classroom,
sit in fire, then flood.

When I cry they don't appear
in their long sweeping robes,
they just leave me to summon
all that I've learned
and turn it outward
as a word, song, or prayer.

SPOTLIGHT

Yesterday morning I spoke with the Sun.
I asked him what he does for work.
He said, "I'm on the lighting crew.
I hold the spotlight for *her.*"
He lifted his chin towards Earth.

From our view in space
we spoke of her beauty –
Her rivers and birds,
her mountains and pearls,
her pure white swirls of cloud.

He reminded me that
those of us who live to serve beauty
must remain freelancers.
"The job is far too important
to be sabotaged by bosses.
It's a good gig," he said,
"What a view from here, huh?!"

"Best job in the universe," I said,
tucking my pen behind my ear,
"Best job ever."

NAVIGATOR

Who said it's easy
to navigate the empire of the insane-sane
where much of what is sold is toxic
and nothing is free?

You must train hard,
keep your mind focused,
your body clean,
recite your formulas and sutras,
find little tricks
to plug up the holes
eaten away by tricksters and fools.

It may take relentless prayer
to keep you afloat
as you tread the seas
of false priorities.
And even then you'll lack structure
to prepare you for another death.

But when you wake up
your dreams will move
in all directions like starlight,
and nothing will tie you down
to the decomposing gears
of this glittering world.

GOALS

It's a sunny Wednesday
and my post-psychosis wellness coach
asks with a snap, clap –
"What are your goals?"

After my "breakthrough"
some words lost all meaning –
words like *alone, tomorrow* and *government.*
Words that didn't survive
the crossing of dimensions.

"What is a goal?," I ask. I'm serious.
Having destroyed the leash the matrix gave me,
having shattered all ceilings of fear and limitations,
having moved through time in all directions,
only to inhabit the present moment,
I don't know what a goal is.

There are dozens of other go-getter words
that seem to have slipped off
the pages of my lips, *praise God.*

Does a peach tree have goals?
A doorbell?
A river?
How about an elephant, as it lifts its mighty tusks
towards the raw canvas of blue sky?

All creatures who lean towards life
do what sustains them.
Sleep, eat, move, make love…
I have no goals.

I am either with or without God.
I am either obeying divine guidance
or overriding vision.
I am in no army or fleet.
The boxes have all been burned.

LIGHT BENDERS

Trauma is the leash that tethers us here.
Why else would you come back
again and again to the Great Mother –
to the medicine in her gutters,
the bandages in her books,
the slivers of love in her rivers
and in all of her reflective surfaces?

Who else in this galaxy
would kiss your deepest wounds?

Lately, my unseen helpers
have been teaching me
how to pass.

This will be the first time
I will leave here intact,
filled with honor,
with a diamond heart,
wearing nothing but
goggles of light.

I'll lift from the body
like fish slipping from skin
to the fields of clear light.
Hallelujah!

I'll no longer need
the Great Wound to keep me here.

No more executions, decapitations
guillotine, noose, injections...*free*.
But that's for when the time comes.

For now, we are entering
the Beginning of the Beginning
so often confused with the Ending.
Our vision is doubled.
The projection upside-down.

It's a birth within life.
There may be tears and confusion.
There may be nights bright as day,
but you'll remember how it's done.

Then when asked –
What do you do for a living?
You can answer
I sing,
walk the Earth,
bend light!

PRISON WARD

When I lay down under a mat black sky
pinpricked with celestial glitter
in a warm nest of dry grass,
the whole prison yard goes silent.

I press my palms to star bursts of straw,
draw sweet ribbons of oxygen in,
feel my skin become nothing.
I'm so dead, I'm alive.

Who is brave enough to take me now,
internally flooded with mute symphonies?

My inmates sit quieter than crickets
wrapped in crisp white ward blankets,
their cigarettes burn orange-red in the dark
marking their one small coordinate
on this home we call Earth.

Can we be each other's saviors?
What color is survival?
Is the concept of a crooked "they"
just "we" in drag?
How many car garages does a blind doctor have?

By day, in the chain link yard,
I trace the shadows of the rooftops
with my sandals
careful not to get too excited about

the unfolding magic of periwinkle flowers
or the liquid poetry of the sun.

Who infected the planet with
miscalculation and greed?
Who taught the darkness
to spin false prophets from
the inaudible songs of the angels?
Who will be held responsible
for this dent in beauty –
its iridescent magic submerged by ego's tide?
Who, in this final hour, will rise above?

EARTH HEART

You are here to help Earth
because the call was made
that the shadows may take us,
leave us charred as night,
and floating through the cosmos
like a burned ball of lost dreams.

Our systems can lose a kidney,
half a leg, a finger or two,
but when the heart is diseased,
life ceases.

Thank the stars you are on a planet
more precious than you know. You see,
there are beings that have descended
that my pen doesn't have names for,
something like the angels of the angels' angels.

They have fought in a Great War and won,
clearing the skies above us,
and inside of us,
whitening clouds,
polishing rainbows,
infusing every raindrop with kisses.

They say, the journey home is always instantaneous
when the senses withdraw and the breath
is invited to land in the sweet fields of bliss.

So have no fear, you're already here,
fully intact. On the New Earth
our support teams have come.
They are working day and night.

Normal is a word where magic doesn't live.

So wish to wake up!
This crisis is a divine transformation.

This twenty minute interview aired on NPR's Blue Ridge Public Radio as a part of "The Porch: Artists Coping with Their Mental Health Through a Year of Turmoil."

Chelsea LaBate has a deep history in Asheville as a musician, songwriter and poet who also teaches the art of songcraft.

Over the past year and a half, LaBate experienced psychotic episodes requiring hospitalization. She now lives with her parents in Florida and is making art inspired by her mental health battles. That's where she spoke with me earlier this month. She began by detailing her mental health journey over the past two years.

~ Matt Peiken

Chelsea: I had never had any sort of depression or mental health issues my entire life. When they started I was 39, so a year and a half ago. I'd just have these larger than life schizophrenic paranoid episodes, that if someone were to see me they would probably say "there goes a crazy person." You know, like full-on talking in different languages, speaking in tongues, not recognizing faces. They kind of have an onramp where before I get paranoid and schizophrenic, I am clairaudient, but then I'm just speaking in tongues and gibberish and little weird high voices. I don't remember those. Those are things people have told me. So

I've had three of those episodes and have been in four mental hospitals.

Matt: Were you in Asheville when that first happened?

Chelsea: I was in Asheville, and I started to have a hunch about which houses had mischievous activities going on in them—and just weird buildings downtown where I was like, why is that door painted shut? Nothing that ever got proven, but that was the experience. I was getting paranoid on behalf of the safety of others.

Matt: So you had never experienced any of this until you were 39? Was there any sense now or in retrospect where you can point to anything that precipitated this or might have tangibly brought this on?

Chelsea: I went through a lot of past lives while I was in the first episode, and I never believed in those. But I actually reenacted them and became who I was in these other lives, to the point where it's like, it became as real as memory, just as real as in this life. So, if that's the truth, and I was beheaded one life and I was hung another life, I was always getting cut off at the throat, which is interesting because I'm an artist and a musician. You know, even if it's dreams you can have bad dreams that you don't remember. That all goes into your one little fragile system and at some point you just have to break out of all of that... break on through to the other side.

Matt: You touched on yourself as an artist which is, I would think, that there is some overlap of your imagination in terms of conjuring imagery in your poetry and your music, versus this kind of imagery. Can you describe the difference? Were you cognizant of those differences?

Chelsea: For those who are artists, there is that moment right before you are writing or singing, like you're feeling it coming down the shoot, maybe, like a frequency—you have your antennae up and you're just receiving it, you're not necessarily generating it—and that's the difference between maybe sitting down and generating a memoir or generating something that was based on things that happen versus receiving and having an antennae to the collective stories, to the collective material, and then you get into other realms. I was talking with galactics. I was talking with ancestors. All these things that before, I just lived my life as an artist and that's where my boundaries were.

I kind of think of it as a keyboard, like a piano. It's like I had four octaves of communication and this was just like, well guess what, we're gonna get all 88 keys now. And I'm like, woah! And that's where the hospitalizations come into play because suddenly you have 88 keys when maybe you've been playing in the Middle C range for a couple of octaves and your vessel can't take it. Your vessel can't harness all of that range and all of those colorations and all of that beauty and all of that horror. It all comes together at once with psychosis. And the beauty is that you do get to touch it.

Even you know, like when you are a kid and you don't really know how to play piano and you just want to run your fingers all the way down and run your fingers all the way up the keys, that's what psychosis felt like to me. It's a matter of overcoming the lunacy factor of it and awakening into wow, I've seen all this color, I've heard, I've experienced, I've tasted all of this color even. The senses start to step in for one another, right? So then the goal is to be able to come back and be able to treat it just like you're sitting there writing a memoir and not be in a place of complete disarray.

Matt: Well tell me, that's a real interesting way to describe the differences, but I would think some artists would see that expanded color palette as "Now I have new things to draw on for my art." It seems like you were very aware that this wasn't normal, this wasn't inspiration. You were aware of that, right?

Chelsea: No, I didn't want to admit that I suddenly had psychic abilities. I didn't want to say that.

That feels like something somebody else would tell me that I have, and I didn't want to say that I was communicating telepathically. I don't know, I just wanted to be an artist, you know, but this is different. I didn't want to claim that or add it to my palette. I was happy enough as I was.

Matt: How did you become aware or accept and absorb that this is an abnormality within you that needed to be addressed?

Chelsea: Great question. Unfortunately I just had to get hospitalized. There's the mania, and I think there can be healthy mania...and other artist friends, you know, I talk to them about that. So it's maybe like you stayed up for two nights straight painting, right, because the lightning is there, it's moving through you, it's there, you have the electricity, whatever, but then you know you can't do that for eight days – you have to eat and you have to maybe sleep for a day, or whatever, but you ride the lightning. That's what mania is – it's a surge of electricity, and I'm still new at navigating when that surge comes through how to harness and capture what it is that I want from the experience. When it gets bad, and this is all of these times that I had these episodes, I wasn't on the right medicines. I wasn't on an anti-psychotic, so I would get into this place where then I would get paranoia. When the paranoia comes, the party is over. There's no making art. There's no "oh this will make a great song." It's ugly, it's dark, it's something that I would never wish on my worst enemy, and that's when I had to go to the hospital.

Matt: Do you voluntarily institutionalize yourself or did it take others in your life to impose that on you?

Chelsea: The first one they took me. They came and found me. I was in my house in Asheville, and I was fighting a great battle, and Joseph Campbell talks about this, Dr. Stanislov Grof talks about this. It's this mythical battle that I had been fighting for maybe three or four days in my home. I hadn't left, hadn't eaten, hadn't drank. I didn't have any sense that I had a body even, and my neighbors put it together along with my parents that I was missing. So they came to my house.

They sent the Asheville police out for a wellness check. And they found me, and I was in the back room, and I had nothing on. The cops came and found me, and then a beautifully patient social worker helped to get me out of the house in a way that wasn't traumatic. So I wasn't put in a straight-jacket. So even though I was psychotic, he helped to get me out and to talk me out of there, and then afterwards my neighbor showed up from next door. She was like "Chels, you can go with me now and I can take you. Or if they have to take you, it may not be fun." I didn't know what was going on, but I knew I had won the battle, and I knew that I was with my neighbor and that I trusted her and I should do whatever she said.

Matt: Where were you brought, and what happened once you were institutionalized?

Chelsea: I was taken to Mission Hospital and I think they hooked me up to some IVs because I hadn't eaten and hadn't drank. I was the color of a school bus evidently. I was jaundiced. There's only X amount of facilities in the state where they can take you for longer term care, and I got taken to a facility out in Hickory, a Duke facility, and was there for two more weeks or so. It's so strange. They never tell you "You're in a mental ward!" I was just like – I'm kind of in a hospital, but it's not really a hospital, and I was trying to put it together. They don't tell you, but I was still in full episode mode. I had to go in the padded cell. They had me in a room confined to myself with no other people for a while. They couldn't really come up with any reason for why I had suddenly gone from 0 to 100.

Matt: So they were treating you in this very isolated, some may say, harsh way in a sense. You had nobody that you felt was an advocate for you. What happened during your time there to lead to you being released?

Chelsea: Just time. And I lied, you know, they were like "Are you hearing voices?" and I said no.

I didn't want more injections, they gave me injections. After X amount of days of sedating me, I guess they finally decided, okay, she can be in her family's home, still needing to be watched, but I would then be cared for by my parents at that point.

Matt: At that point when you were released, you were brought to Florida?

Chelsea: Yes, I was brought to Florida.

Matt: So that was the first of what you said were three episodes that happened in the past year and a half plus. Obviously there was time in between each episode when you're not having these psychotic events. Tell me what would happen, in your experience, to bring them on.

Chelsea: That's what we're still trying to figure out, because I'll feel fine and suddenly I'll start spinning out. And they say to look for your triggers, right? You know your triggers can be this, your triggers can be that.

Matt: How long do these episodes last for you?

Chelsea: They're months. I mean, it's like the revving up is maybe a month or so, but then the actual episodes are maybe two weeks—where I'm feeling that heightened sense of communication, that I am communicating with spirits and galactics and having this ongoing conversation. It just feels like my nose turned on, you know. Imagine if you didn't smell and then suddenly your nose turns on, and then you're like "Oh! Well I guess this makes sense that I could be able to do this." So that's what it feels like. It just feels like these other senses turned on that are in the family of the creative arts. It's that same antennae. It's so fascinating because I'm like yah, I've been doing this my entire life, but not really. I mean there are songs that I fully channeled.

Matt: Are there any lessons that you've come to know now in your experiences with these episodes and the revving up for you to recognize the difference between, "Oh, this is creative inspiration and oh, this is revving up to what's not going to be a great time for me? Or is it all just a mesh for you in that you don't know you're in the revving up process, versus the creative process, until it's too late?

Chelsea: Yes, until it's too late. That's where I am right now. The first three were like – it's just too late, because it happened so quickly, and/or because the revving up process is so slow and it feels so well integrated that it doesn't feel like a threat, it just feels like – Oh! Now I'm awake! My senses are turned on. These senses. Suddenly I can dream. Suddenly I can imagine. Suddenly I can receive messages that are going to help me to be healthy and whole.

Matt: How have your experiences in the past year and a half to almost two years had any impact at all on your artistry or your desire to create?

Chelsea: I faced my own mortality multiple times in the past year and a half, but hands down I am addressing death point blank. It's there in the lyrics, it's there in the words in a way that I'm not running from it and I'm not, *not* mentioning it. It's the same with going nuts. Like one poem I have is called "Madness," and it starts off with me taking off my dress and leaving it on the floor because I know I'm about to be reborn or I'm gonna die and I want to cross over with the dignity and with the proper dress of someone who is doing that.

Matt: So you're still making music, you're still writing poetry directly informed by these experiences that you're having, and also you're still in the throes of this, it seems like. Correct me if I'm wrong, but you have not discovered nor have you received any sort of medical help beyond certain drugs, perhaps to help give you a key to what's happening with you?

Chelsea: No, and we're just patching it all together. Like even this morning my mom and I had these psychiatrist lists, and I have a counselor that's okay. It's just they want to pathologize everything, you know? Psychosis is medicine. And I don't think anyone has said that before I have, and that's why I am putting it in the poetry, right? It's like you can go through the files and just rip them up and throw them out and just have them in front of you and then you're done. It's a release. It's a process that is holy, I think. But it's not sustainable.

Matt: Explain that a little bit, when you say psychosis is medicine.

Chelsea: Well, if your psyche had a junk drawer in it, right, and all that stuff is just rattling around, and finally you just can't take it anymore and you know, it opens up, it needs to be cleaned out, we're going to another place together. And in order to do that, you can understand how to have those releases in a way that doesn't cause severe episodes like I've been having, or you can have the episode and the episode will do it for you. I'm not more injured because I've had three psychotic episodes. I'm in a much better place. I'm not afraid of death. I'm so easy going now. I don't have this big pressure chamber of all of this old data.

Matt: Are you saying there has been a positive to these episodes?

Chelsea: Absolutely. And they've been beautiful. I've come into contact with spirit, the divine, the one, the voice, whatever you want to call it and have had direct correspondence. When I was in the hospital the first time, there was nothing there that was sustaining me but the voices that I could hear. And people are like, "Oh, you're hearing voices... injection time." But we all hear voices. If you're an artist, you hear voices. It may not sound like my voice coming out of my mouth, now, but it's more of an impressionistic communication. You might hear the voice of the way the leaves look. It might be more of a visual voicing, if that makes sense. This is like a call to clarify. Can you harness the lightning? And this is what we have in other cultures, we just don't have it here. Our culture doesn't have it because we are voice-a-phobes. You know, it's like you can't be hearing that. Well, how did the wise men find Jesus? They didn't have GPS! They followed something.

Matt: Are you saying that for you the way you want the people around you to handle and treat this is not by institutionalizing you but to be bumper guards in a way to make sure you stay within the lane of not harming yourself or other people, but let you experience these episodes of your own volition?

Chelsea: I can be manic and not be totally insane. It's the insanity, that no, I have to go to the hospital. I may hurt people. I need the meds. As of now.

Matt: I would imagine when that happens with you, your grasp on reality isn't clear at all and you must feel that everybody is against you. That's that paranoia.

Chelsea: Ooh yah. It's bad. And when you're in one of those scary places and you think they're against you and you think the dark side is coming for you, it really is an absolute challenge to maintain a level of peace.

Matt: What would you recommend to people, anywhere, who either have friends or family who from their vantage are experiencing these psychotic episodes? How should they behave and work and treat their loved ones?

Chelsea: Well, one thing that I would love, that no one has ever really asked, maybe after they've gone through the episode – ask them what they experienced. Did they become Jesus? Were they walking on water? There is some really powerful narrative that I experienced and went through that was holy. I mean it was beautiful and no one ever asked me about it. It all just gets watered down into, "Did you take your meds today, and are you hearing voices?"

Matt: I'm impressed and awed that you are creating work in the midst of such a personally calamitous time for you and doing work that is directly drawn from this. What do you intend for that work? Is it just for you or are you planning or wanting to put this out into the world?

Chelsea: I so want to put it out into the world in a bigger way. The collection is 52 poems. My working title is "Corona" and it's long format poems, so I am really hoping that this will go out in a way that can really invite people into the experience. I want people to feel invited into psychosis.

If you or a loved one is struggling with mental illness, please contact:

the National Alliance on Mental Illness, for weekly free groups on Zoom and in person, as well as information and education on mental health.

Nami.org

To hear these poems read by the poet herself in video form, please become a patron at: patreon.com/tencentpoetry

Author Bio

Chelsea Lynn LaBate is an award winning
songwriter, poet, painter, book binder, runner,
surfer and yogi. She has played thousands of shows
for the global community, including performances
for children and elders.

She has released several albums, animated music
videos, and a podcast for songwriters called
Songcrafter, which aired on the radio as an hourly
Saturday morning special. She has a collection of
short love poems called "Sugah" which she hand
bound into miniature wearable books.

She lives a simple life by the sea, in New Smyrna
Beach, FL, helping others with her words and
making her art.

MEZCALITA
PRESS

An independent publishing company
dedicated to bringing the printed poetry,
fiction, and non-fiction of musicians who
want to add to the power and reach
of their important voices.